Happiness and Marriage
by Elizabeth Towne

Start Publishing PD LLC
Copyright © 2024 by Start Publishing PD LLC

All rights reserved, including the right to reproduce this book or portions thereof in any form whatsoever.

Start Publishing PD is a registered trademark of Start Publishing PD LLC
Manufactured in the United States of America

Cover art: Shutterstock/Taisiya Kozorez

Cover design: Jennifer Do

10 9 8 7 6 5 4 3 2 1

ISBN 979-8-8809-0530-0

Table of Contents:

Chapter I: To Be Happy Though Married 6

Chapter II: A Tale of Woe 10

Chapter III: To Be Loved 14

Chapter IV: The Pharisee Up-To-Date 16

Chapter V: So near and Yet So Far 19

Chapter VI: Marriage Contracts 24

Chapter VII: Some Hints and a Kick 28

Chapter VIII: The Heart of Woman 33

Chapter IX: The Law of Individuality 37

Chapter X: Harmony at Home 40

Chapter XI: A Mystery 42

Chapter XII: The Family Jar 44

Chapter XIII: The Truth about Divorce 46

Chapter XIV: The Old, Old Story 49

The inner side of every cloud Is bright and shining;
I therefore turn my clouds about,
And always wear them inside out— To show the lining.
        —James Whitcomb Riley

And I will show that there is no imperfection in the present,
  and can be none in the future,
And I will show that whatever happens to anybody it may be
  turned to beautiful results.
        —Walt Whitman

Chapter I: To Be Happy Though Married

"Some dear relatives of mine proposed Ada as my future bride. I like Ada and I gladly accepted the offer, and I mean to wed her about the middle of this year. Is this a working of the Law of Attraction? I want to make our married life happy and peaceful. I long for a wedded life of pure blessedness and love and joy without even a pinhead of bitterness ever finding lodgment in our household. How can I attain this state of peace? This is what I now do: I enter into the Silence daily at a particular hour and enjoy the mental picture of how I desire to be when married. Am I right? Please tell me how to make my ideal real." Tudor, Island of Ceylon.

The above letter comes from a member of the Success Circle who is a highly cultured and interesting looking native East Indian. We have a full length photo of him in native costume.

He asks if "this is the working of the Law of Attraction." Certainly it is. Just as the sun acts through a sheet of glass so the Law of Attraction acts through the conventionalities of a race. Whatever comes together is drawn together by the Law. Whatever is held together is held by that same Law of Attraction.

This is just as true in unhappy marriages as in happy ones. If two people are distinctly enough individualized; that is, if they understand and command themselves sufficiently; their attraction and marriage will bring to them only pleasure. If they are not distinctly enough individualized there will be a monkey-and-parrot experience whilst they are working out the wisdom *for which they were attracted.*

When soda and sour milk are drawn together there is a great stew and fizz, but the end thereof is sweetness and usefulness. So with two adverse and uncontrolled natures; but out of the stew comes added wisdom, self-command and rounded character for each.

When each has finished the work of helping the other to develop they will either find themselves *really* in love with each other, or they will fall apart. *Some stronger attraction will separate them at the right time*—perhaps through divorce, perhaps through death.

All our goings and comings are due to the Law of Attraction. The Law of Attraction giveth, and it taketh away. *Blessed* is the Law. *Let* it work. And forget not that *all* things are due to its working.

This does not mean that the Law has no way of working *except* through the conventionalities of a people. Many times the attraction is to break away from the conventional. *The stronger attraction always wins*— whatever is, is *best* for *that time and place.*

"Tudor" says he "enters into the silence daily at a particular hour and enjoys the mental picture of how he desires to be when married."

His success all depends upon the *equity* in that picture; upon its truth to the law of being.

An impractical idealist lives in the silence with beautiful pictures of "how he desires to be when married." When he gets married there isn't a single detail of his daily experience which is like his mental picture. He is sadly disappointed and perhaps embittered or discouraged.

It all depends upon the picture. If Tudor's picture contains a benignant lord and master and a sweet little Alice Ben Bolt sort of wife who shall laugh with delight when he gives her a smile and wouldn't hurt his feelings for a farm; who does his bidding before he bids and is always content with what he is pleased, or able, to do for her; if this is the style of Tudor's mental picture he is certainly doomed to disappointment.

I have a suspicion that Tudor is a natural born teacher. His mental pictures may represent himself as a dispenser of moral and mental blessings. He may see Ada sitting adoringly at his feet, ever eager to learn. If so there will certainly be disappointment. East Indian girls may be more docile than American girls; East Indian men may be better and wiser lords and masters; but "Ada" is a Human Being before she is an East Indian; and a Human Being instinctively revolts from a life passed in leading strings. If Tudor continues to remind her that he is her schoolmaster she will certainly revolt; inwardly if not outwardly. Whether the revolt comes inwardly or outwardly harmony is doomed.

The first principle of happy marriage is *equality*. The second principle is *mutual confidence*, which can *never* exist without the first.

I do not mean by "equality" what is usually meant. One member of the married twain may be rich, the other poor in worldly goods; one an aristocrat, the other plebeian; one educated, the other unschooled; and yet they may be to each other what they are in *truth*, equals.

Equality is a *mental state*, not a matter of birth or breeding, wisdom or ignorance. The *truth* is that *all* men and women are equal; all are sparks of the One Life; all children of the one highly aristocratic "Father"; all heirs to the wisdom and wealth of the ages which go to make up eternity.

But all men and women are more or less unconscious, in spots at least, of this truth. They spend their lives "looking down" upon each other. Men "look down" upon their wives as "weak" or "inferior," and women look down upon their husbands as "animals" or "great brutes." Men are contemptuous of their wives visionariness, and women despise their husbands for "cold and calculating" tendencies.

Every man and woman values certain qualities highly, and in proportion as another fails to manifest these particular qualities he is classed as "low," and his society is not valued.

This is the great source of trouble between husbands and wives. Each values his or her own qualities and despises the other's. So *in their own minds* they are not equal, and the first principle of harmony is missing.

The real truth is that in marriage a man is schoolmaster to his wife *and she is equally schoolmistress to him*. This is true in a less degree, of *all* the relationships of life.

The Law of Attraction draws people together *that they may learn*.

There is but one Life, which is growth in wisdom and knowledge.

There is but one Death, *which is refusal to learn*.

If husbands and wives were equals *in their own minds* they would not despise each other and *refuse to learn* of each other.

The Law of Attraction, or Love, almost invariably attracts opposites, and for their own good. A visionary, idealistic woman is drawn to a practical man, where, kick and fuss and despise each other as they will, she is bound to become more practical and he more idealistic. They exchange qualities in spite of themselves; each is an unconscious agent in rounding out the character and making more abundant the life of the other.

Much of this blending of natures is accomplished through passion, the least understood of forces. And the children of a union of opposites, even where there is *great* contempt and unhappiness between the parents, are almost invariably *better balanced* than *either* of the parents.

I cannot believe that unhappy marriages are "mistakes" or that they serve no good purpose. The Law of Attraction draws together those who need each other at that particular stage of their growth. The unhappiness is due to their own foolish *refusal* to learn; and this refusal is due to their contempt for each other. They are like naughty children at school, who cry or sulk and refuse to work out their problems. Like those same naughty children they *make themselves* unhappy, and fail to "pass" as soon as they might.

Remember, that contempt for each other is at the very bottom of all marital unhappiness. The practical man despises his wife's impulsive idealism and tries to make her over. The wife despises his "cold and calculating" tendencies and tries to make him over. That means war, for it is impossible to make over *anybody but yourself.*

Because the man despises his wife's tendencies and she despises his, it never occurs to either to try making over *themselves*, thus helping along the very thing they were drawn together for.

If Tudor's picture holds two people who are *always* equal though utterly different; whose future actions are an unknown quantity to be taken as they come and each action to be met in a spirit of *respect* and inquiry, with a view to understanding and learning from it; if over and through all his picture Tudor spreads a glow of *purpose* to preserve *his own* respect and love *for her*, at all costs;—if this is the sort of picture Tudor makes in the silence he will surely realize it later.

It requires but one to strike the keynote of respect and personal freedom in marriage; the other will soon come into harmony.

You can readily see that all marital jars come from this lack of equality in the individual mind. If a man thinks he is perfectly able to take care of and to judge for himself he resents interference from another. On the other hand if he believes his wife is equally able to judge for *herself*, he *never* thinks of interfering with her actions. Of course the same is true of the wife. It is lack of respect and confidence which begets the making-over spirit in a family, and from this one cause arises all in harmony.

Individual freedom is the *only* basis for harmonious action; not only in marriage but in all other relationships of life.

And individual freedom *cannot* be granted by the man or woman who considers his or her judgments superior to the judgments of another. A man *must* accord his wife *equal* wisdom and power with himself, else he *cannot* free her to act for herself. A woman must accord her husband that same equality, or she *cannot* leave him free.

It is human (and divine) nature to correct what we believe to be wrong. Only in believing that the other "king (or queen) can do no wrong," lies the possibility of individual freedom, in marriage or out.

The man or woman who knows he or she is believed in and trusted is very careful to *deserve* that trust. Did you know that? The sure way to have your wishes consulted is to exalt and appreciate the other party. Did you know that a man or woman will cheerfully sacrifice his or her own opinions in order to retain the respect and love of the other? But if he thinks the respect and love of the other party is growing less he will give free reign to his own desires.

Married people "grow apart" for the one reason that they find fault with each other. Of course it begins by their being disrespectful to each other's faults, but it soon develops into disrespect of each other. From "looking down" upon a husband's faults it is only a few short steps to looking down upon *him*. His faults keep growing by recognition, and his good points keep shrivelling for lack of notice, until *in your mind* there is nothing left but faults. From trying to make him over you come to despair, and give him up as an altogether bad job.

And there isn't a grain of sense in all this madness. Stick to the *truth* and you will get rid of the madness and the friction, too. The truth is that your husband, or your wife, would be an egregious *fool* to follow your judgments. You don't know beans from barley corn when it comes to the actions of anybody but yourself. The One Spirit which enlightens *you* as to *your* actions is also enlightening your other half as to *her* actions; and do you suppose this Spirit is going to favor *you* with better judgment about your other half's duties, than it has given *her?* I guess *not*. Don't be presumptuous, my boy. Do you own little best, and *trust* your other half to do hers. Trust that she *is* doing the best.

And above all trust the One Spirit to run you both.

If you do this your wife will *rise fast* in your esteem. And the higher she finds herself in your esteem the harder she will try to please you— and rise higher.

And, girls, don't forget that the shoe fits equally well the other foot. Either man or wife can bring harmony out of chaos simply by *respecting* the other half *and all his or her acts*.

A marriage without "even a pinhead of bitterness" is a marriage without a pin-point of fault-finding, mental or oral.

Chapter II: A Tale of Woe

"Why is it that, in more than two-thirds of families the wife and mother bears not only the children but the burdens and heartaches? The husband supplies the *money* (generally not enough), the wife has the care of a growing and increasing family, the best of everything is saved for 'Father' and he is waited on, etc. If the children annoy him he goes to his club; if the wife dies, why there are plenty more women for the asking. Thousands of women are simply starving for Love and men are either willfully blind or wholly and utterly selfish. You possibly know that this is quite true. Another thing that has caused me many a time to question everything: During the Christmas holidays many times I have seen half-clad, hungry, shivering little ones gazing longingly into the wonderful show windows, wanting probably just one toy, while children no more worthy drive by in carriages, having more than they want. Love, home, mother, everything; on the other hand hunger, want, blues (many times), and both God's children. Let us hear what you have to say about this." B. B.

Why does the mother in two-thirds of the families bear not only the children but the burdens and heartaches? *Because she is too thoughtless and inert not to.* It is *easier* to submit to bearing children than it is to rise up and take command of her own body. It is easier to carry burdens than to wake up and *fire* them. It is easier to "bear" things and grumble than it is to kick over the traces and *change* them. To be sure, most women are yet under the hypnotic spell of the old race belief that it is woman's duty to "submit" herself to any kind of an old husband; but that is just what I said—women find it easier to go through life half asleep rather than to *think* for themselves. Paul says a woman is *not* to think, she is to ask her husband to think for her. (At least that is what the translators *say* Paul says. Privately, I have my suspicions that those manly translators helped Paul to say a bit more than he meant to.) It is *easier* to let her husband think for her even when she doesn't like his thoughts. So she uses her brain in *grumbling* instead of thinking.

People who don't think are ruled by *feeling*. Women feel. They feel not only for themselves but for other people. They shoulder the burdens of the whole family and a few outside the family. They do it themselves— because it is *easier* to feel than to think. Nobody walks up to a woman and says, "Here—I have a burden that's very heavy—*you* carry it whilst I go off and have a good time." No. The woman simply *takes* the burden and hugs it and "feels" it—and *prides herself on doing it*. And maybe the thing *she* hugs as a burden is no burden at all to the other people in the family. My dear, women as a rule are chumps. They'd rather feel *anything* than to *think* the right thing.

Now I'd like to know if you think a woman who has made herself round-shouldered and wrinkled and sour-visaged over burdens—*anybody's* burdens, real or fancied—is such a creature as attracts love or consideration from *anybody*. Of course she is not. It is no wonder she receives no love or consideration from her husband or anybody else. She has made a pack mule out of herself for the carrying of utterly useless burdens that nobody *wants* carried and the carrying of which benefits nobody; and now that she has grown ugly and sour at the business she need not feel surprised at being slighted. And she need not blame folks for slighting her. *She* assumed the burdens; she carried them; *she* wore herself out at it; it is all her own fault. It was *easier* for her to feel, and grumble, than to wake up and *think*, and change things.

Nobody who *thinks* will carry a single burden for even a single day. He knows that fretting and worrying and grumbling only *double the burden* and accomplish nothing.

Woman has *built herself* for bearing children and burdens. When she gets tired of her bargain she will *think her way out of the whole thing*. In the meantime the harder the burdens grow the more quickly she will revolt and make of herself something besides a burden bearer.

It is all nonsense to talk about the men being "willfully blind or wholly and utterly selfish." No man *wants* a burden-bearing, round- shouldered, wrinkled and fagged-out wife. No man respects or loves a woman who will "submit" to bearing unlimited burdens or babies either. And if a woman "submits" and yet keeps up a continual grumbling and nagging about it, a man simply despises her.

What every man *hopes* for when he marries a woman, is that she will be a bright, trim, *reasonable comrade*. If she is even half-way that she will get all the love and consideration she can long for. But in three- quarters of the cases of marriage the woman degenerates into a whining bundle of *thought-less feelings* done up in a slattern's dress and smelling like a drug-shop. Her husband in despair gives up trying to understand her, or to love her either.

The woman in such a case is apt to suffer most. Why not? *She makes it the business of her life to "suffer."* She *prides* herself on how much she has had to "suffer," and "bear." She cultivates her "feelings" to the limit. A man thinks it "unmanly" to *give way* to "feelings." So he uses all his wits to keep from doing so, and to enable him to hide his own disappointment and make the best of life as he finds it.

A man uses his best *judgment* when he meets disappointment. A woman trots out her "feelings" and her best pocket-handkerchief, and calls in the neighbors. So the woman gets the lion's share of "sympathy"—which means that all the other women get out *their* best handkerchiefs and try to imagine just how *they* would "feel" if in her place.

Of course there *are* exceptions. I *have* heard of men who wept and retailed their woes; and I have heard of women with gumption.

The woman who wrote the letter at the head of this chapter is a feel-er, not a thinker. She looks at the forlorn, bedraggled specimens of her own sex and "*feels*" with them, never *thinking* that the women themselves have anything to do with making their conditions. She "feels" with the woman because *she* is a woman. Being an unthinking creature she cannot "feel" for the man at all.

Woman is the weaker creature for no other reason than that she lives in her "feelings."

Man is the stronger for no other reason than that he uses his wits and his will to *control* his feelings. "B. B." has seen children gazing into shop windows. Immediately she imagines how *she* would "feel" if in their places. She does not stop to *think* that in all probability the simple act of gazing into the window may bring more real joy to those children than the *possession* of the whole windowful of toys would bring to some rich man's child. She does not *think* that life consists not in possessions or environment, but in the *ability to use* possessions or environment. If she were an Edwin Abbey or a Michael Angelo she would gaze on our chromo-bedecked walls and work herself up into a great state of "feeling" because we had to have such miserable daubs instead of real works of art. If she saw us gazing on an Abbey or Angelo picture she would weep tears to think we couldn't have such pictures instead of those hideous bright chromos on our walls. It would never occur to her that we might be privately comparing her Abbeys and Angelos with our chromos, *and wondering how anybody could possibly see beauty in the Abbeys and Angelos.*

About nine-tenths of women's so-called "sympathy" is just about as foolish and misplaced as that. If "B. B." would go up and get acquainted with some of those small youngsters she sees gazing into the shop windows she would find some of her illusions dispelled. She would find among them less "longing" than she thinks, and more wonder and criticism and pure curiosity—such as she would find in her own heart if she were gazing at a curio collection.

I remember a large family of very small boys that I used to "feel" for, very deeply. Poor little pinched, ragged looking fellows they were, and always working before and after school hours. I gave them nickels and dimes and my children's outgrown clothes, and new fleece lined gloves for their blue little hands. They kept the clothes hung up at home and the gloves stuffed in their pants pockets. And one day I discovered that every one of those small youngsters had a *bank account*—something I had never had in my life! They lived as they *liked* to live, and I had been harrowing my feelings and carrying their (?) burdens for nothing.

This world is *not* a pitiful place. It is a lovely great world, full of all sorts of people, every one of whom *exactly fits into* his conditions.

And the loveliest thing of all about this bright, blessed old world is that there is not a man, woman or child in it who cannot *change* his environment if he doesn't like the one he now occupies. He can *think* his way into anything.

A real, deep, tender feeling will prompt one to do all he can to alleviate distress or add to the world's joy. *Real* feeling prompts to action. But this sentimental slush which slops over on anything and everything in general is nothing but an imitation of the real thing. To sympathize to the extent of *acting* is good; to harrow up the feelings when you cannot or will not act, is simply weakness.

"Feeling" is subject to the same law as water. Take away its banks and it spreads all over creation and becomes a stagnant slough of despond. Confine it by banks of *common-sense* and *will* and it grows deep and tender and powerful, and bears blessings on its bosom.

The professional pityer is adding to the sum total of the world's misery.

The world is like "sweet Alice Ben Bolt"; it laughs with delight when you give it a smile, and gets out its pocket handkerchief to weep with you when you call it "Poor thing!"

Then it cuts its call short and runs around the corner to tell your neighbor what a tiresome old thing you are anyway.

Never you mind the tribulations you can't help, dearie. Just wake up and *be* the brightest, happiest, sweetest thing you know how to be, and the world will-be that much better off.

Chapter III: To Be Loved

"I desire to attract love from the Infinite or somewhere, that I may not be starved for it, as I have been ever since I married. My husband sneers at the New Thought, and in fact at nearly all that is best in me."

Caroline.

And yet this woman has children to love her. She thinks she is in need of being loved; but what she really needs is *to love*. Being loved is the *effect* of loving. A loving man or woman can never want for love. Others turn to them in love as naturally as flowers turn to the sun.

In order to be loved you must *radiate* love. Instead of trying to attract the love of others, seek to *give* your love to others, *expecting nothing in return*. After a time you will find the unexpected coming to you spontaneously.

Learn to love by loving *all* people and *things*, and especially all things you find to do.

This same Caroline wants to "rise above drudgery." What *is* drudgery? *It is simply unloved work*—nothing more nor less. *Any* work which is looked down upon, and which is done with the hands *whilst the heart and mind are criticizing it*, and running out after other things,—*any* work thus done is drudgery. Work done with the hands *and a small and unwilling part* of the mind, is drudgery. To her who *respects*, and *loves*, and does with a will what she finds to do, there is no drudgery.

Let the woman who longs to be loved begin to *love*, by practicing on her work. To quit calling it "drudgery"; to put *all* her mind and will and *soul* into *each* piece of work as it comes; is the first and longest step toward loving it. It is an easily demonstrated fact that we learn to love anything we persist in doing with a whole-souled will.

To love our work enlarges our capacity for loving people, and the more we love people, *and the more people we love*, the more radiant we become.

It is the radiant lover whom all the world loves. Do you know that love and the lack of love are governed by "auto-suggestion"? It is *natural* to love, as every child does. But as we grow up we keep saying to ourselves (this is auto-suggestion, you know) that we "don't like this," and we "don't like that," until really we *shut up* our love and live in a continual state of "don't like"—a state which in due time develops into *hate*—hate for self as well as others. "Don't like" does it all.

Now *cultivate* love by auto-suggestion. Keep saying, "I *like* this," and "I like that." *Hunt* for things to like, and even tell yourself you like things when you don't *feel* that you like them at all.

Feeling is a *result* of suggestion. Nothing easier to prove than that. A hypnotist can, by suggestion, make you feel almost anything, whether it is true or not. He will say, "You feel sad," and straightway you will feel so. Then he will say, "You feel happy," and you do. Your feelings are like a harp, and your *statements*, or auto-suggestions, are the fingers which pick the strings. Take good care to play the tunes you *want*—to say you *like* things, or love them. Then you will quickly respond and *feel* that you like or love them. Keep *practicing* until you love *all* the time. Then you will *be* loved to your heart's content.

Chapter IV: The Pharisee Up-To-Date

As long as you continue to hug the delusion that you are "not to blame" for the unpleasant things in your conditions you might just as well profess the old thought as the new. The very fundamental principle of mental science is the statement that *man is a magnet and able to attract what he will.* To repudiate this statement is to knock the props out from under the whole philosophy. Better stay an old-thoughter and let Jesus suffer for your sins and those of your relatives and friends. At least Jesus *took* the sins of the world to bear, all of his own free will. There is some comfort in letting Jesus do what he chose to do.

But you have turned away from Jesus as a scapegoat. You refuse to lay your burdens on him who offered to bear them; and you refuse to bear them yourself. Instead you distribute them around among your relations and friends and then fret your soul because they won't accept your distributions. Of course you excuse yourself by acknowledging "your share of responsibility" for the unpleasantness of conditions, but if you will examine carefully you will find that your portion of the responsibility includes most of the *good* things in your conditions, whilst you have portioned off almost *all* the responsibility for the *bad* things among your protesting—or indifferent—relatives. You always say, "*I* try so hard," but you never balance that with, "*He* tries so hard,"—"*They* try so hard." You get all the I-try-items in your own pile and the don't-try-items in other folk's piles. "*If* it were not for Tom and Dick and Harry and Fan you would do wonders—*if* they'd only treat you with *half* the consideration other people give you, or half *they* give other people!—*if!*—*if!*"

I wonder why they don't indeed! It is just because you are you, *and you attract your own particular kind of treatment.* To all intents and purposes Tom, Dick, Harry and Fan are a punch and Judy show and *you pull the strings.* When other people pull the strings there's a different sort of show. You are the motive power in *all their treatment of you.* Not a tone or look or act of theirs in your direction but *you* are responsible for; it was *you* and no other who drew them to you; and it is you and no other who hold them there.

Now don't say, "I don't see *how!*" Of course not—*you haven't wanted to see how*—you've been too intent justifying yourself. And anyway, it takes an open mind, and some time, and much *faith* to enable us to see the *principles* of things. We have to *act* as if they were so, a long time before we see that they are. If you had *acted* upon the principle that you are a magnet and that *all* that comes to you comes by your attraction, you'd have long ago had your eyes opened to "see how." And you'd have made progress and *changed your conditions.*

If you are ever going to be a magnet you are one now. If you are ever going to be able to attract to the hair's breadth whatsoever you will *then you are doing it now*. There will be no miraculous change in the running gear of this universe to enable you to attract what you want.

What you now are in essence and working principle you have always been, and you will always be—the same yesterday, today and forever—a self-made magnet, working to the hair's breadth.

Only by Changing the Quality of Your Magnetism Can You Change Your Environment and Attract Different Treatment from Tom, Dick, Harry and Fan.

Sweetness within brings sweetness without. You have been more or less bitter and self-justifying within, and Tom, Dick, Harry and Fan have danced to the strings you pulled.

As long as you think *you* try and they don't; as long as you think *your* judgment superior to theirs; *your* ideals loftier and worthier; *your* ways better; you will get from them responses of carelessness, bitterness, lack of consideration, selfishness.

You are inconsiderate of *their* ideas, ideals, judgments and ways; *in self-preservation* they are inconsiderate of yours. If you had your way they'd be pretty little putty images of *your* ideals, judgments, wishes, ways and feelings. The Law of Individuality prevents your imposing yourself on them. You think you are finding fault with *their* "lack of consideration"; *you are really condemning the law of being.*

If you are ever to be a magnet you are one *now*. *All* that comes *is* "your fault." If anything different comes it will come through *your* change of mental attitude and action.

It will not do to throw it on "Karma" either, and say you are receiving now the unpleasant things deserved in a previous state of existence. The mills of the gods grind slowly but they are not so dead slow as all that. What you thought and did in a previous state has determined your parentage and childhood environment in this. But the pangs you suffer today have their roots in yesterday or day before, or the year before that. Cause and effect trip close upon each other's heels—so close that the careless or ignorant observer misses the trip. He exaggerates the *effect* if it be an unhappy one, and goes nosing for a bigger cause than the real one. How could *his* little slip of this morning, or yesterday, be the cause of this *terrible* evil which has befallen him?—and he slides completely over the real cause. *And keeps on repeating it.*

Self-righteousness, by blinding your eyes to the truth, is the direct cause of the most gigantic and the most subtle miseries of the world. These awfully good people who fully realize how hard they have always tried to do right, are the unhappiest people in the world—unless I except Tom, Dick, Harry and Fan, the victims of these self-righteous reformers. No, I can't even except these; for they at least generally succeed in having their own way in spite of the would-be reformer. But what so utterly disheartening as continued *lack of success*? And the self-righteous one never succeeds. It is hard, *hard*, to be so wise and willing, with such *high* ideals (the self-righteous one is strong on ideals), and *never* to succeed in making Tom, Dick and Harry conform to them. Do you see why Jesus said so often, "Woe comes to the Pharisee"—the self-righteous? And why he called them hypocrites? Of course they are unconscious of their hypocrisy—self-righteousness blinds them to the truth;

they think *others* are to blame for most of the self-righteous one's own hard conditions.

The self-righteous one is doomed to a tread-mill of petty failures. He goes round and round his own little personal point of view and learns nothing.

It is by getting at the *other fellow's* point of view that we learn things—about him and ourselves, too. When the self-righteous one wakes up to the *fact* that the world is *full* of people whose points of view are *just exactly* as right and wise and ideal as his own; and begins to *feel with*, and *pull with* these other people, instead of against them; when he does this he will find himself out of the treadmill to *stay*. As he shows a disposition to consider *other* people's ideals and help others in the line *they* want to go, he will find the whole world eager to help *him* in the way *he* wants to go. The self-righteous one works alone and meets defeat. The one who, recognizing his own righteousness *in intent*, yet forgets not that *others are even as he,* is the true friend and *be*-friended, of all the world.

Now don't let this homily slip off *your* shoulders. We are *all* self-righteous in spots, and none of us is so *very* wise that he cannot by self-examination and readjustment learn a lot more.

Each soul *in its place* is wisest and best. Don't *you* try to get into the pilot house and steer things for Tom, Dick, or Harry. Stay in your own and steer clear of the rocks of anger, malice, revenge, *resentment, resistance, interference* and *immoderation*.

Chapter V: So near and Yet So Far

"Help me to make things go forward instead of backward. I want to be neat and attractive, with a good head of hair, a good complexion and good health. I want to help my husband so he will fall in love with me to make home beautiful, attractive and comfortable. I want bright eyes and freedom from that careworn look. Oh, I want to draw my husband nearer to me." (From a Taurus woman, aged twenty-seven.)

Isn't that pitiful? And heaven knows—or ought to—how many poor women, *and men, too,* live with that same dumb longing to get nearer and be chums with somebody. That cry touches my heart, for I lived years in the same state.

And, oh, how I struggled to draw others nearer to me. How I agonized and cried and prayed over it. How I worked to make home attractive. How I cooked and washed and scrubbed, sewed and patched and darned to please! How I quickly brushed my hair and hustled into a clean dress so as to be neat and ready when my husband came in! And how I ached and despaired inwardly because he frowned and found fault! How I studied books of advice to young wives! How their advice failed! How I *tried* and *tried* to get him to confide in me and make a chum of me! And how the more I tried the more he had business downtown! Oh, the growing despair of it all! And the growing illnesses, too! Oh, the gulf that widened and widened between us! Oh, the *loneliness*! Oh, the *uselessness* of life!

I *had* to give it up. I wasn't enough of a hanger-on to sink into a state of perpetual whining protest, or to commit suicide. When I was finally *convinced* that I *couldn't* draw him nearer I gave it up and began to take notice again, *of other things.* I let him live his life and I took up the *"burden"* of my own "lonely" existence.

And the first thing I knew my "burden" had grown *interesting,* and I was *no longer lonesome.* I began to live my life to *please myself,* instead of living it for the purpose of *making over* the life of another.

The *next* thing I knew my husband didn't have so much business downtown, and he had more things he wanted to tell me. I found we were nearer than I ever dreamed we'd be.

You see, I had become *more comfortable to live with.* I had quit *trying* to draw him nearer, and behold, *he was already near.*

In the old days I lived strenuously. I hustled so to get the house and the children and myself *just so,* that I got *my aura* into a regular snarl. My husband being a healthy animal, felt the snarl before he saw the immaculateness; and like any healthy animal he snarled back—and had business downtown. He responded to my *real* mental and emotional state, responded against his will many times; and I did not know it. I supposed him perverse and impossible of pleasing. I *knew* *I* had tried my best (according to my lights, which it had not occurred to me to doubt), but it never entered my cranium that *he* had tried, too. I looked upon the outward appearance—my immaculate appearance, met by fault-finding or indifference I Poor me! Perverse he!

Poor Martha, troubled about many things, when only one thing is needful—a quiet mind and faithful soul. History does not state if Martha had a husband. If she did, he was perpetually downtown. And Jesus preferred Mary, the Comfortable One, to Martha. Poor lonesome Martha! And she tried *so hard* to please.

I used to know a woman who never did a thing but look sweet. She was pretty and sympathetic and *cheery*. Her husband and six children idolized her, and fairly fell over themselves to please her and keep the home beautiful for her. There was physical energy galore lavished *gladly* by the family, in doing what is commonly considered the mother's work.

And there was apparently nothing whatever the matter with that woman, who was always sweet and pretty as a new blown rose, and looked not a day over twenty. She was simply born tired and wouldn't work. Of course the neighbors said things about her; but nobody *could* say things *to* such a sweet tempered, cordial and pretty woman. And there'd have been razors flying through the air if anybody had dared hint to that husband or one of those children that mother was anything less than perfection. The family explanation was that "mother is not strong."

But that mother did more for that family than all the others put together. *She made the atmosphere*, and she was the life-giving sun around which husband and children revolved, and from which they received the real Light of Life—the power which develops the good in us.

The mother's main business in life was that of *appreciating*. She was the confidante, the counselor, the optimistic teacher, and the appreciative audience for six children and a husband, besides a lot of neighbors who carried their troubles to her. She performed more mental work than it takes to manage a billion dollar trust. She kept six children, not only out of mischief, but *happily busy* at all sorts of household and outdoor work which it was well for them to know. They learned to keep house and farm by keeping them, whilst she sat by and enthused and directed their efforts. She made them *love* it all. She helped them over the hard places in their school work and enthused them to do better work. They carried off the school prizes under her admiring eyes, and ran straight to lay them in her lap and receive that proud and happy smile of hers.

Her husband worked like a slave *with the heart of a king*. She thought him the best, bravest, brightest of men, and told him so a dozen times a day, besides *looking* it every time he came in range of her big, loving brown eyes and smooth, rosy cheeks.

I never heard of an unkind word in that family, and those six children grew up into splendid young manhood and womanhood. Their mother is still the blessed sun of their existence. She is prettier, healthier and happier now, and so proud of her fine children.

And she is *up-to-date*. She has studied and read with her whole family and is interested with them in the world's present events, art, literature and religion.

Happiness and Marriage

Do you think that woman ever complains of loneliness, or "tries so hard" to draw husband or children "nearer"? No. She long ago chose the "one thing needful"—*a faith-full heart*. Her physical strength would not bear much strain without depressing her faith-full-ness; therefore she left the physical labor out, *as less important*. To her the *Life* was more than meat or raiment, so she ministered to the Life—to the joy of living. A stronger woman, physically, could have ministered more efficiently to the physical side without neglecting the "one thing needful." This woman chose the better part and stuck to it; and *results* prove her righteousness.

The foolish woman looketh upon the outward appearance and is troubled over *many* things. She wears herself out trying to keep the *outside* immaculate and grieves her heart out because she misses the one thing of great price, the *joy of loving and being loved, of trusting and being trusted*.

Do you know that we are *never* far away from *anybody*? We are close, *so close* to our husbands; our children; our friends; *even to our enemies if we have them;* and to those we never saw or heard of. *We are all One. Your* soul is *my soul too*. Only our bodies are at all separated, and they are separated *only as the harbor is separated from the sea*. Our bodies are but inlets of One Great Soul; and they are but the smallest part of ourselves. Is it then not foolish to *try* to draw another nearer? Why, we are *now* so near we *can't* be nearer; we are *One*. Why strive to do what is *already* done?

Ah, you see, we work from a false hypothesis. We are so concerned with the many things on the *outside* that we lose sight of *inside truths*.

Take your husband's nearness for granted. Be not troubled over the many things of appearance. *Have faith in him*. If there is any "drawing nearer" to be done see that *you* draw near to him *in faith and love*. Instead of mentally or verbally sitting down on his motives, words or acts, *try to feel as he does, that you may understand him*.

As we geow in understanding of another we grow in love and realization of our nearness to that one. In proportion as we dislike or are repelled by any person or his actions, in that proportion we fail to understand him.

As one human being is revealed to another the sense of nearness grows. Now do you imagine that distrust and censure will help a soul reveal itself? Of course not. But if you can be comfortable and indulgent to a man, and especially if you can cultivate a real admiring confidence in him, he will unfold his very heart of hearts to you. It is *you* who must come near in faith and love, if you would find your husband near to you.

To sum up:

1. You and your husband *are* close together—so close you are *One*.

2. If you would *feel* the truth of this you must come to your husband in faith-full love, and you *must not allow yourself* to condemn or judge, verbally or mentally, his revelations of himself. You must vibrate *with* him where you can, and *keep still in faith* where you can't understand him and meet him.

3. You must persist in thus doing, until faith and love and understanding become the habit of your life.

4. The same rules apply if you would feel your nearness to any other person, *or to all persons*.

Every man is in embryo a good and thoughtful and loving husband. A wise wife will give him the loving, full-of-faith, appreciative atmosphere which encourages development.

"We are all just as good as we know how to be, and as bad as we dare be." *And we are all growing better.* Why not chant the beauties of the good instead of imagining it our "duty" to eternally bark against the bad?

It is said there cannot be a model husband without a model wife, and *vice versa.* True. Then if yours is not a model husband *don't assume that you are a model wife fitted to judge and admonish him.*

Be still and get acquainted with him.

Make it your *first* object in life to cultivate a serene and faith-full heart and aura.

As a means toward this end cultivate a *full* appreciation of whatever and whoever comes near you. Cultivate the spirit of praise; and *trust* where you cannot see.

Second, take *good* care of your body and personal appearance. Allow plenty of time for bathing, caring for your hair, nails, teeth, and clothing. Wear plain clothes if need be, but *don't* wear soiled or ragged ones. And don't ever put a pin where a hook or button ought to be. No man can continue to love a woman who is slatternly.

Third, allow at least an hour *every* day for reading and meditating on new thought lines, *and for going into the silence. Let nothing rob you of this hour, for of it will come wisdom, love and power to meet the work and trials of all other hours. Remember the parable of the ten virgins and take this hour for filling your lamp, that you be ready for the Unexpected. Only in such hours can you lay up love, wisdom and power which will enable you to make the best of the other hours. Let not outward things rob you of your source of power.*

Fourth, unless you wish to fall behind the world's procession see that you spend some time every day in reading the best magazines and newspapers, taking pains to skip most of the criminal news. Read optimistically and cultivate a quick eye for all the good things. Take the *best* magazines even if you have to leave feathers off your hat and desserts off your table. If you can find an *interesting* literary club it might be well to join it and do your part of the work. But see that you do not *rob* the Peter of your energies to pay the Paul of club ambitions.

And fifthly comes your housework. This is the juggernaut department which grinds many a woman to skin and bones—and her husband discards the remains! When it comes to housekeeping a woman has need of all the love, wisdom and power she can muster in her hours of silence. Even a five room flat or cottage is more than one woman can keep *spotless* and allow time for anything else. Many things *must* be left undone. The wise woman simplifies to the last degree compatible with comfort. Useless bric-a-brac is dispensed with. "Not how much but *how good,*" is her rule when buying. A few good things *kept in place,* are better than a clutter of flimsy things which pander only to an uncultured esthetic taste—and make work. *Order* is the wise woman's first law in housekeeping; cleanliness her second, which is like unto the first in importance. She lets extra rooms, furniture and fallals go *until she can pay well to have them cared for.* The same rule obtains in her kitchen and her personal dress.

The wise woman thinks of comfort and allows time for the *joys* of life, wherefore *all* her life is a pleasure.

The foolish woman is ground under the wheels of routine. To her, housework is a stern "duty" which comes *first*, and to which body, mind, personal appearance, happiness, the joy of living, all must be sacrificed.

Lastly, firstly, and all the time, the wise woman is guided in what to do and in what to leave undone, by the Spirit of Love; whilst the foolish woman is guided by the Spirit of Appearances.

Note the order in which I have written these needs of life; an exact reversal of the usual order. Housework *last*, and the Spirit of Comfort first. The tendency of every woman is to lose *herself* in troubling over the many things of her household. If she would be happy, useful, young and growing she *must* turn her life the other side up.

The best way to begin, the only successful way so far as I know, is by *Making* time for the hour of reading and meditation and silence. She must *take* the time, by sheer force of will—take it until it grows into a habit which *takes her.* Out of this hour will come first peace and self-control; and gradually she will find unfolding out of this peace and control, the wisdom to know what to do, and how; and what *not* to do. From this unfolding comes the *only* power which can make new thought practical to the individual case.

Are you satisfied with yourself and your condition? Then pursue your old ways.

Are you dissatisfied with yourself and surroundings? *In order to change them* you *must change—that which was first with you must become last* and the last must be first.

Be still and know the I *am* God of you; and, lo, all *things* shall be added. But the *things* must be last, not first.

Seek ye *first* the kingdom of Good in yourself, *and to be right with it*; and all things shall be added. All things shall be added to *you*, not to *other things.*

Be still until you find yourself—your wise, loving, joy giving Self which dwells in the silence and is able to do whatsoever you desire.

Chapter VI: Marriage Contracts

"That article of yours, 'So Near and Yet So Far,' has worried me to an extent I am ashamed of. To my 'judgment' that article is disingenuous. It is not so much that you jumped on that poor soul with hob-nailed shoes, but that you formulated the 'jump' quite as the husband might have done. That is, if *she* would repent and change her course, she would soon find that *he* was all right, and—inferentially—all the trouble was of her making. Not one word on the other side! You even quote your own experience *against* her. My dear, *did* you really find that your 'trouble' was of your own making, and *did* you really change *anything* except your own amount of distress during the process of disintegration? Marriage is the only contract which society does not promptly admit to be broken when either party refuses to fulfill his obligations—as agreed to. And in view of the custom of ages, and the instinct in woman formed by such custom (when instinct makes the establishing of Individuality the *very* hardest thing in life for a generous woman), I think that your implication against the woman, trying with all the light she's *got* to keep her side of that very one-sided contract is simply—cruel! I wish I could get at that girl and tell her that her *only* chance for happiness is through the paradox 'Whoso *will* not lose his life *cannot* find it.' Whoso will not 'let go' of the love which his five per cent judgment claims as his only *righteous* chance, cannot inherit that which the ninety-five per cent would attract if the five per cent were 'offered up' to the spirit. This is the first time I have ever disagreed with your point of view." Jane.

That article, "So Near and Yet So Far," has brought forth volumes of comment, most of it highly favorable, and nearly all of it from women themselves. But among the writers were three critics, and among the critics one of the brightest women I know, whose letter appears above.

And she says that article is to her disingenuous. Of course it is, for she has not yet arrived at the point of *giving up her own way*. She is still a Pharisee of the Pharisees—on the surface. She is proud; she *knows* she has done her best to bring things right—according to her judgment of right; and she *does hate* to acknowledge her foolishness! She will "hold fast her own integrity" as long as there is a shred of it left! Don't I know? Didn't I do exactly the same thing? Of course. But the pressure of the great spirit of love, wisdom, justice, was too much for me; I *had* to give up my judgment; I *had* to acknowledge that there *must* be the same spirit expressing in my husband's judgment; I *had* to let go, be still and get at *his* point of view. Jane, too, will have to do it. And the fact that that article "worried her to an extent she is ashamed of," is the proof. When Truth presses her point we worry until we can hold out no longer; then we give in.

One of the other two critics writes that over that article she "shed the first tears in over seven years." Then she asks me if I don't think I was a "little hard on the Taurus woman," and goes on to reveal plainly that her tears were those of *self-pity*. Don't I know? Haven't I shed quarts of such tears? Of course.

But not more than an ounce or two were shed after I gave up my own way. But this second critic is arriving just as I did, and as Jane will—arriving all unconsciously to herself. Her letter sounds like a chapter from my own thinking of a dozen years ago. She gives a bird's eye view of her husband—no, of her husband's *faults*; she tells how she reads new thought literature on the sly—just as I did; and she winds up with this *piece* of good advice:

"I will say to such, live your own life as God intended you to, regardless of the fact of your husband. Be brave, hope, will and pray. Dress, look sweet. If your husband tells you he doesn't care how you look but to not come near him with your foolishness, as mine does, why, let him live his life in his own way, make home attractive for your own sake, read good books; and in time books will be your chum."

The third critic, too, is full of self-pity, though she does not mention her tears; and her letter is a long portrait of her husband's faults. She wants a little encouragement to leave him, but she is afraid he will go to the dogs if she does. So, like a generous woman, she sticks to him and makes the best (?) of a bad bargain.

Jane says my article was "cruel." Dearie, it was—as the surgeon's knife is cruel. But it is the truth, and it hurts but to make way for healing. The woman who blames has in her eye something worse than a cataract. The woman who sheds tears over her "fate" is moved by the "meanest of emotions." She attracts "cruelty," not only from that article, *but from her husband.*

It takes *two* to quarrel, *and either one can stop it.* It takes *two* to maintain "strained relations," and *either one can ease the strain.* The principles I tried to elucidate in that article are as applicable to a man as to a woman. But it was a woman, a Taurus woman, who asked me; therefore I talked straight to her. And *I* am a Taurus woman who has been through the same mill; and I wrote not from a hardened heart but from one made tender by experience and the Spirit of Truth. My point of view "might have been the husband's" *if* the husband had been an unusually just one. And I must say the husband's point of view is more apt to be *just*, than the wife's; for the reason that a woman is more apt to be blinded by *emotional self-interest.* In proportion as man or woman is ruled by emotion his judgment is distorted. *As a rule man's judgment* is straighter than a woman's. But judgment is a shallow thing, based upon *already revealed facts.* Woman's intuition goes to the heart of things and flashes facts into revelation. Women as a rule *see farther*, but are apt to misjudge what is *close at hand.* Only as man wakes in woman and woman in man do right judgment and love commune. Why not judge with the husband, as I *feel* with the wife? Is any man *totally* depraved?

Jane feels abused because she thinks *I* think that in family strains the woman is more at fault. *In a sense* I do. *Women cannot only make and unmake empires but they* do *make or fail to make harmony* at *home.* Why, men with all their power are mere rag babies in the hands of women of *tact.* Women are the *real* power in the world—the power behind the throne. If only they would develop that particular kind of power instead of coming around in front of the throne to lay down the law!—instead of measuring their *man*-strength against man. Real *woman*-strength will move the most stubborn of men. If I "blame" the woman *(I blame neither, any more than I blame a child for childishness)* it is because *I know she is the ruling power.* Her responsibility is determined by her real power.

And above all a Taurus woman may rule her home—*and does.* Either she rules by force—for she has more than her share of the man in her—and makes war and trouble for herself and others; or she learns her lesson and rules by *loving tact*; in which case her husband rises up and calls her *blessed.* The *woman who knows and rules herself* is the woman of Proverbs XXXI, 10th to 31st verses. Her husband is honored among men *because he is honored at home*; and because he is honored he *lives up to it.* Why, girls, you hold your husband's destiny in the hollow of your hand, in a far greater sense than any man holds a woman's.

But as I said before, *it takes two to make an unhappy home and either one can bring harmony out of discord.* Any ordinary woman can do it *if she will.* And any extraordinary man can do it quite as well as an ordinary woman.

This is not a question of what "society" admits; it is a personal question between one man and one woman. It *is* a partnership, whether society so admits or not. And the failure of one of the partners to live up to the expressed or implied agreement does not justify the other party in the misdoing of her part *as long as they live together.* Does one theft or murder justify another? No! Neither does a neglectful husband justify a scolding or spiteful wife, nor *vice versa.*

Two people marry *first*, for the happiness of love; and second, for home privileges. No matter whether love flees or not, *as long as they keep up* the home-privileges partnership it should be done in the spirit of harmony. Remember, it takes *two* to destroy harmony and *either one can restore it.* If marriage is not a love contract let it at least be a harmonious business contract. If you can't, or won't, *adjust yourself* to your husband, then leave him. Don't stay and half-do your part of the business and cultivate hate and contempt. It's hell. *Get out.*

I have known several couples who lived years in comparative happiness after love had flown; who were kind to each other, considerate, business-like. The wives made pleasant homes and the husbands came and went at will. In their spare time the wives developed their personal interests and "lived their own lives," as critic number two advises. When the husbands took cranky streaks the wives simply made light of it to themselves, and forgot it as soon as possible. They lived on as comfortable terms as if the wives were simply *first-class* hired house-keepers; little crankisms were all in the bargain. Eventually every one of these couples separated, and nearly all the parties are now *happily* married. *And every couple parted amicably*; each being *satisfied* to terminate the old partnership.

To me a divorce is not a disgrace, but a family row *is.* And I suspect that most divorce *rows* are worked up to *drown guilty consciences.* Neither has done his best by the other, and he knows it; so he raises a great row to fix attention on the other's shortcomings that his own may escape observation.

Until a man and woman have succeeded in living up to their home privileges in a manner befitting honest and intelligent man and woman, *they can't be sure that they are not fitted for a real loving union.* Friction over small things obscures vision and judgment, and hate hides the lovableness that *must* lie in every being. Get rid of the rowing over little things of every day life, and you will be able to love as much as your marriage will permit; *and you will be free to dissolve the entire partnership if you desire.*

Did I *really* change anything? *Yes.* Is it "anything" to bring peace and quiet pleasure and comfort and appreciation where their opposites were wont to hold bacchanale? *Yes.*

No woman who *honestly* tries the course I have endeavored to outline will ever doubt that she really accomplishes *something*; neither will she regret.

Here is a word every married woman will do well to heed as long as she lives with her husband: *If you can't have your way without a fuss, then try his with a good will.*

Peace be unto you; peace, which is the foundation for *all you desire.*

Chapter VII: Some Hints and a Kick

"And now, Elizabeth, let me suggest something. Punch up the *men* a little in the matter of cultivating cleanly habits, etc. Women are preached to eternally on these matters and the men wholly neglected. It would be a 'new thought' to take to the men a little and might assist in making more of them fit companions for the sweet and cleanly women they delight in associating with. The absolute neglect of the masculine sex by writers on these subjects causes them to think that nothing in the way of the aesthetic is expected of them. It is a wrong to the men not to en-me and make me his chum as well as his wife. Help courage them to aspire to a common plane with woman in the matters of purity and cleanliness. Cleanliness is next to Godliness, but no more so in the case of woman than of man. It is time for equality to be recognized in this matter as in all others." Carrie.

It is funny how many women squirm when reminded that it is they who set the pace in the home! We are always longing for power and a field of effort, and then when a 20th century prophetess arises and tells us we *are* all but almighty, and shows us how to direct our almightiness to accomplish results, we—well, we squirm. One would think some of us are a little bit ashamed of the pace we have been setting, of the things we have been accomplishing with our almightiness! You know, our first impulse when we see an error in our own selves is to sound the trumpet and charge upon the error in the other fellow. Is this why Carrie wants the men scolded?

Well, *don't* they get scolded? What are their wives and daughters and sweethearts for but to scold 'em or coax 'em into cleaner ways of living? No use to talk to men as a class, about anything but politics. Don't you know that Adam couldn't even taste an apple until Eve coaxed him? Adam is a great theorizer; he will gaze at an apple and tell you that he ought not to eat it, and *why* not; he will even amble long and wishfully about that apple; but it takes *Eve* to wake in him the *living impulse* to take it. Just so with matters of personal neatness. He knows—oh, yes, knowing is his long suit!—he knows he "ought" to be neat; and he thinks he wants to be; but unless Eve and the serpent come along he hasn't the *living impulse*.

And Eve must not lose sight of the serpent, however far away the dove may fly. Eve must use wisdom and tact, as well as example; if she would have Adam accept her standard of cleanliness she must see to it that her example is *beautifully* clean instead of *painfully* so. There are men who are careless about their persons simply as a matter of relief from the painful cleanliness of their surroundings.

Then there are Adams who are careless for lack of interest in pleasing Eve. In these cases you will find that Eve has little or no interest in pleasing Adam; or that she overdoes the matter of trying to please, and frequently dissolves in tears and precipitates countless reproaches upon luckless Adam.

Then there are Adams who are careless from petty spite—with shame I say it. And with greater shame I say, you will find their Eves are spiteful, too;

probably more spiteful than the Adams; for Eve, you know, is generally smart enough and ambitious enough to outdo Adam in any line of endeavor—especially in the use or misuse of the tongue.

In matters of niceness it is Eve who sets the pace. Adam is built for strength; Eve for beauty and adornment. It is *natural* for Eve to set the pace and for Adam to follow, in all matters of detail and niceness. Whether Adam follows with good grace or ill depends upon Eve and the serpent. If Eve is wise as the serpent in her, and harmless as the dove in her, she can lead Adam a *willing* captive to heaven or hell.

Now will you rise again and—squirm—because I attribute to Eve all power over Adam? Will you say I excuse Adam's transgressions and come down hard on Eve? I suppose so. But the very fact that you resent the imputation is proof that in your heart of hearts you know I have hit *very close* to the mark. When an arrow flies wide we are merely amused at the poor marksmanship; but the closer the arrow strikes to the center the more excited we grow—either with resentment or admiration, according to our sympathies.

In matters of cleanliness, niceness and adornment Eve sets the pace; and if her pace is a graceful one and *not too fast* Adam follows. In due time he *acquires the habit* of doing the little ablutions and adornings Eve has taught him.

If your Adam is *very* careless about these matters you may depend upon it that when he was growing up his mother was either dead or careless or tactless; and you may safely suspect that Adam in his previous state of existence was a forlorn old bach. So be gentle with him, for it will take time to correct the faults of such an Adam.

But don't give up, Eve, dear. Be gentle, but be firm and persistent. Use your ingenuity in finding ways to make Adam *want* to please you; and if you can look back over a year or two and see that he *has* improved in *some* respects at least, that there are even one or two little tricks of niceness which have become almost if not quite habitual, then hold a little praise meeting and rejoice. Praise him for learning, and praise yourself for what you have succeeded in teaching him. And if your success has come *without friction*, if you have inspired Adam to *want* to please you, then glorify yourself exceedingly—*all to yourself, of course*. If you let Adam know you are managing him even for his own good, he will show his independence by going back to his old tricks—just as *you* would do if in his place. If there has been friction, or lack of success, let it wake you up to use henceforth *more of the wisdom and love which is in you*.

Now this little homily is written ostensibly to women; but all my men subscribers will read it and applaud. *I wonder how many of them will see that every word of it is as applicable to themselves, as to their mothers, sisters, sweethearts, wives?* Every Eve is Adam at heart, and every Adam is Eve; and what in sauce for Adam will prove equally effective with Eve. Adam and Eve are both green, and growing. They are the two halves of a ripening peach, brought together by the Law of Attraction or Love because at this stage in their development *they fit*. You will be inclined to doubt that every Adam's nature fits his Eve's, but I say unto you judge not according to outward appearance but judge righteous judgment. Now listen:—Every human being has his manifested good points and his *latent* good points. The manifest good points of a man are the Adam of him; the *latent* good points—the weak places in him—are the Eve of him—the interior as-yet-undeveloped part of him. The strong points, the good points, of a woman are the Eve; the weak points, where she is as yet undeveloped, are the Adam or interior nature of her.

If it were not for personal attractions, particularly the attractions of one man and one woman, the *latent* parts of both men and women would remain forever undeveloped and their strong points would continue to grow stronger. In time (supposing the race did not die out), there would be two classes of people utterly different and at variance with each other—two opposites with no understanding or sympathy for each other.

Attraction brings together opposites; the strong, steady man falls in love with a frivolous butterfly; a handsome woman attracts a homely man and *vice versa*; a strong, capable woman marries a sickly, incompetent man—and supports him; a sentimental woman is attracted to a matter-of-fact man who develops her common sense by pruning her sentimentalities; an artistic temperament is drawn to a phlegmatic; a sanguine to a bilious; a mental to a vital; an active man marries a lazy wife, or *vice versa*; a bright man marries a stupid girl; and so on and on.

Man and wife are a rounded whole in which the man manifests what is latent in the woman, and the woman supplies that which in the man is as yet undeveloped. Just as Eve coaxes, or scolds, Adam into habits of neatness; as Adam coaxes, scolds or drives Eve into having his meals on time, thus developing her self-command and *promptness*; so they act and re-act upon each other to develop a thousand latencies of which they, and the onlookers, are more or less unconscious.

The foolish Adams and Eves fret and strain against these processes of development, and bewail their "mistake" in marrying; not seeing that the association is really benefiting both. The wise Adams and Eves reduce the friction *by kindness*, by *co-operation with each other*; Adam *tries* to please Eve, Eve tries to please Adam, and both are kind about it, wherefore in due time their *appreciation* for each other grows, and mayhap their love grows with it. If love wanes instead of growing at least they are *friends*, and can *part* as friends if they so desire.

Someone has well said that without a model husband there can be no model wife. I believe it. As long as man and woman are held together by love, attraction, or "conditions" (in its last analysis it is *all* the Law of Attraction, or *God*) they are literally *one*, no matter how hard they kick against the oneness; and neither man nor woman can *alone* be a model, any more than one side of a peach can be *entirely* ripe and sweet and the other side entirely hard and green.

So when I speak to Eve about tact and kindness I speak to *the Eve in Adam* as well as in Eve herself.

And what I say of the attractions of man and wife applies equally well to other family relationships, to friendships, to acquaintanceships and even to our relationship to the people we pass on the street or *the heathen we never saw*. Every person who touches us even in the slightest degree, *is drawn by the law of attraction because we need him to bring out some latency in ourselves, and because* he *needs us to help develop some latency in him.* It is our own highest desires (the god in us) which constitute the attraction.

"Oh, but *that* can't be," you exclaim, "because So-and-So brings out only the *evil* in me. He makes me feel *so* hateful and mean." Let us see, dearie. *The hateful and mean feelings are due to your* resisting *that which his influence would bring out of you.* For instance, you were late at your appointment with him. Of course you *thought* you had a good excuse; but if promptitude were *one of your strong points,* instead of one of your latencies, you would have been on time in spite of that excuse—if it were your *habit* to be on time you'd have swept aside a much greater hindrance before you would have allowed yourself to be behind time. Now So-and-so is naturally prompt and, having had some experience with you he knew you were not; so when, he having arrived fifteen minutes ahead of time as it is *his* nature to do, *you* came tripping in fifteen minutes late—smiling confidingly as you excused yourself (he, having spent the half hour in cultivating a grouch at you for not being as prompt as himself)—he, of course, looked sulky and answered shortly. Then you pouted and finally *worked yourself* into quite a temper over his inconsiderateness and crankiness because of that paltry little fifteen minutes he had to wait. He *worked himself* into a temper because you were not on time; you *worked yourself* into a temper because he wasn't "nice." All that working was your individual doings.

But it all resulted in your resolving that if ever you had another engagement with that man (you'd take good care not to if you could help it, though!) you'd be *on time* if it killed you. Of course you didn't tell him so. And *he* resolved that the next time he made an engagement with you he'd know it, but *if* he did he would make up his mind to be *on* time instead of ahead of time, and he'd not care if you *were* late.

So you see, the Law of Attraction accomplished its divine purpose in attracting you two to make that engagement—it waked in you a *resolution* toward promptness; and it waked in him a *resolution* to be *on* time rather than *before* time in future, and to be civil if you happened to be late—since you are only a woman and can't be expected to appreciate the value of promptness!

This is the way all our associations in life work together for good *to develop our latencies,* to strengthen our weak points. *The wiser we are the less emotion we waste in resenting the developing process—the more readily we see the point and take the resolution hinted at.* You see you and your friend had had other such experiences as the one described—you had been late before when So-and-so condoned the matter and said nothing. *He let you off so easily that you never thought of resolving not to be late again.* You *felt* that he had been displeased but you depended upon your niceness to make it all right again, and it never occurred to you to call yourself to account and *resolve* that it should not happen so again. You were *too heedless* to take a hint, so you had to have a kick.

You may set this down as a rule without exceptions: *That all the kicks you get from relatives or friends come after you have ignored repeated hints from your own inner consciousness and them.* You have gone on excusing yourself *without correcting the fault* (perhaps without seeing it) until the Law of

Attraction stopped hinting and administered a kick. And if *one* kick will not cause you to develop that weak point the Law of Attraction will bring you other and yet harder kicks on the same line. *You will attract* worse experiences of the same sort.

It is this very law which makes married folks (or other relatives or friends) quarrel. Adam refuses Eve's *hints* about neatness, and Eve kicks—harder and harder. Eve refuses Adam's hints and he gets to kicking. *It always takes two to start the kicking*, and either one can stop it. *A frank acknowledgement of error and a resolution to mend your end of the fault no matter what is done with the other end; then a pleasant expression and no more words;—this will stop the kicking. And in proportion as you learn to take the hints you attract, you will cease to attract kicks.*

By all of which I am reminded of that old testament statement that *'the Lord hardened the heart of Pharoah.'* The "Lord" or "Lord God" of the old testament is what I call the *God in us*, or the Law of Attraction in us; and the "God" of the Bible is The Whole—the God *over all* as well as *in the individual*. It is the *God in us* which attracts to us our experiences, *in order to teach us wisdom and knowledge*. Pharoah was not *wise* enough to let those people go, so the God in Moses gave him a hint—which he failed to take. Wherefore he attracted a gentle kick in the way of a plague. This dashed his ardor a bit and he gave permission for the Israelites to go; but he was only *scared* into doing it; and after the plague was called off he was not wise enough to keep his word—here was a great lot of valuable slaves which he *could* keep, and why shouldn't he?—his word was easy broken and all's fair in business; so *his heart hardened* and he held the Israelites. So he attracted a harder kick; which failed to accomplish its purpose. Kick after kick came, each a bit harder than the last; each scaring Pharoah for the moment, but *none convincing him*. He still thought it *right* to hang onto his slaves if he could, and he had the courage of his convictions. A man of such splendid courage seems worthy of a better fate. Pharoah had the courage of a Christ, coupled with the ethics of a savage, whose only law is his own desire of possession. Because he could not take the hint and *see his mistake*, he attracted a series of kicks increasing in power until one finally landed him in the Red Sea. Perhaps a glimmer of the truth reached him as the waters rolled over. But his soul goes marching on and his mistakes are still re-incarnating here on earth.

Is Adam kicking, Eve? Take a hint before he kicks harder. Is Eve making things warm for you, Adam? Take care you jump not out of the frying pan into the fire. Are circumstances plaguing you, Everybody? Take the hint lest worse plagues arrive; learn wisdom and avoid the Red Sea.

Be not wise in thine own conceits. *Lean* not upon thine own understanding, but in *all* thy ways *and thy neighbor's ways*, acknowledge that the One Good Spirit leads, and He shall direct thy feet in paths of peace and pleasantness.

The proof of foolishness is unrest and friction.

The proof of wisdom is peace.

Be still and know the Lord thy God, and learn from what He draws to thee.

Chapter VIII: The Heart of Woman

"My wife has fallen in love with another man. She keeps house for me and I am trying to show her all the love I can but it seems to have no effect upon her. I love her dearly and desire to win her back. What should be my attitude toward her and toward the man?" A.J. (who is one of many who have thus written me.)

Goodness knows! *Be* good and you will know. In other words, be just to all three before you are generous to anybody. Of course that is not easy to do, but it is possible; and it is the only thing you can never be sorry for afterward.

First, get down to first principles. There are three *individuals* concerned—three separate and complete beings, each with his inherent right of choice. Nobody *owns* anybody else; nobody "owes" anybody else anything in the way of "duty." Each individual stands on his or her own two feet and makes an effort at least to go where he or she will find the most happiness.

Every one of these three Individuals has made mistakes—he or she has thought happiness was to be found in this place, or that. He or she has made the choice and trotted on his or her two feet to this place or that, only to find happiness was not there as he or she supposed. *We don't always know what is for our happiness.* But goodness knows!—and *all* our mistakes work together for ultimate happiness.

In the truest sense there are *no* mistakes; a mistake being simply a case where things failed to come out as we calculated. *They came out right nevertheless.* That is, they came out right for our enlightenment. By them we grew in wisdom and knowledge. Next time our judgment will be better.

The wife in this case no doubt thinks just now that her marriage to A.J., was "all a terrible mistake." If so she is making another "mistake." That is, she is thinking what "ain't so." Whatever experiences she has had with A.J. were drawn to her by herself, for her own enlightenment and development. They were all *good*.

It *may* be that she and A.J. have gained from their association all there is in it. Doubtless the wife thinks a separation and a new marriage would make her supremely happy. May be it would. May be her judgment is right this time.

On the other hand it may be wrong, as it has been oft before. Many a woman has jumped out of the frying pan of one marriage into the fire of another.

Only time will tell. If this new love is the "soul mate" she thinks, the attraction will be all the stronger and steadier in a year or two from now. If he is not the soul mate she thinks him, the attraction will wane.

I know women who, under similar conditions, have elected to wait; women whose consciences would not allow them to leave a kind husband or young children for the sake of gratifying their passion for another man. I have known these same women to despise a year or two later, the men they had thought themselves passionately and everlastingly in love with. They have never got over thanking whatever gods there be that they were saved from that rash step. I have known *many* cases of this kind, and have received many letters of fervent thanks from both men and women who followed my private counsel to *let time prove the new attraction* before severing old ties and making new ones.

And I must say that *not one* who waited but has said to me, "I am *glad* I waited"; *whilst many who did not wait have bitterly regretted.*

A love affair is emotional insanity. Lovers are insane; not in fit condition to decide their own actions. The state of "falling in love" is moon-madness. For the time being the lover's sense of justice, his reason, his judgment, is distorted by *reflections from another personality.* This is especially so in the woman's case, for the reason that she is generally a creature of untrained impulse, instead of reasoning will.

There is that recent case of the beautiful and beloved Princess Louise who ran away from her royal husband. She thought she loved Monsieur Giron so devotedly that she could bear anything for the sake of being with him. And surely she was miserable enough in her old environment. But when it came to the reality she could not bear the consequences. She wanted her children; her proud spirit winced at the snubs she got; she longed a little for the old life; and familiarity with her soul mate revealed the knowledge that he was not *all* soul. She flunked miserably and went home to her sick child. You see, she was literally love-*sick.* Her mind was disordered; a life spent with her soul mate loomed to her so large and dazzling that all other things were as nothing. She couldn't for the time being see straight. She was literally insane.

If she had only *waited* until the new wore off her passion! Waited until she saw things in their proper proportions and relations to each other; until she was *sure* she could *live the life* made inevitable by her change.

That is the trouble;—love-sick-ness *blinds her to the truth.* When she wakes up by *experience of the truth, she wishes she hadn't.*

The only safe thing for a woman to do who finds herself married to one man and in love with another is to *wait,* a year, or two or three years, until time proves her love and *she knows in her heart* that she can make the change and never regret it, no matter what happens. *You see, she can never be happy with the new love as long as* conscience or heart *reproaches her for her treatment of the old love.* It behooves her to consider well.

Time will prove the new love. In many such cases times reveals the idol's feet of clay. He shows that his love is for *himself,* not for her. He pouts and kicks and teases like a petulant child. He wants her *now,* no matter how she may suffer in consequence of his haste.

In spite of herself, in spite of her love for the new love, she finds he is not panning out as she supposed. She begins to see his other, his everyday side—the side she will have to live with *if she goes to him.*

Now is the husband's chance. She *knows his* every-day side, from experience; she has tried it in weal and woe. If he rises to this occasion the Ideal Man, he stands a fair chance of winning from his wife a *deeper* love than she has yet given any man. He may catch her *whole* heart in its rebound from the idol with feet of clay.

To a husband in such a position I would say, *Be kind.* "There is nothing so kingly as kindness!"—and true kindness under this most trying condition will in time win even a recalcitrant wife's admiration and love—*if the two are really mates.* If they are not real mates; if they have outgrown their usefulness to each other; the sooner they part the better. To hold them together would only be another "mistake."

Because a man and wife were mates five or ten years ago is no proof that they are mates today. We are all *growing,* and it is often literally true that we "grow away" from people.

Every loved one who goes out of our lives makes room for a better, fuller love—unless we shut ourselves in with our "grief."

It is said that Robert Louis Stevenson fell in love with the wife of his best friend. He told his friend frankly, intending to leave the city. His friend questioned the wife and found she reciprocated Stevenson's love. Stevenson stayed with his friend in Paris and the wife went to her father's home in California. A year later, the attachment between his wife and Stevenson still remaining, the friend applied for a divorce. Then he and Stevenson journeyed all the way to California together, where Stevenson was married to the ex-wife. The ex-husband attended the wedding, and that same evening announced his engagement to a girl friend of Mrs. Stevenson.

I glory in the friendship of those two men who refused to allow the unreasoning caprices of love to sever their love for each other. A separation and remarriage like that is a *credit* to all parties concerned. *It is the quarrels and estrangements which are the real disgrace* in cases of separation and remarriage.

John Ruskin was another man too great and too good to resent love's going where it is sent. He had married, knowing that her respect and admiration but not her *love,* were his, a beautiful and brilliant girl much younger than himself. They lived happily a number of years. Then Ruskin brought home the painter, Millais, to make a picture of his wife. Artist and model fell in love. Ruskin found it out, and refused to allow his wife to sacrifice herself for him. He divorced her and gave her to Millais, and the three were life-long friends.

If I were a man in such a case as A. J.'s I should treat my wife as I would a daughter. I would treat her as an Individual with the right of choice.

Many a daughter has rushed headlong into a marriage which her relatives opposed and she regretted at leisure.

If someone grabs you by the arm and pulls hard in one direction you are forced to pull hard in the opposite direction, or lose your balance and fall. If a daughter is pulled away from the man to whom she is attracted, her Individuality rebels and she pulls toward him harder than she would if let alone. She *chooses* to follow the attraction which at the time is pleasanter than that between herself and her frowning relatives.

Remembering this I would *free* daughter or wife and trust to the God in her to work out her highest good. I would *believe* that whatever she chose to do was really for her highest good. If I *really* loved *her* I would *prefer* her happiness to my own.

And in it all I should be *deeply* conscious that whatever is, is best, and that *all things worked together for my best good as well as for hers.*

Whatever appearances may show to the shortsighted, the real *truth* is this:—*Justice reigns; the happiness of one person is not bought at the expense of another; the law of attraction brings us our own and holds to us our own in spite of all its efforts to get away; it never leaves us until*, through some change or lack of change in ourselves, *it has ceased to be our own.*

A man's "mental attitude" toward the other man in such cases as A.J.'s should be the same as toward other men—the attitude of real kindness toward an Individual who, like the rest of us, is being "as good as he knows how to be and as bad as he dare be."

This does not mean that the husband shall allow himself to be used for a door mat, nor held up for the ridicule of the neighbors. A sensible father expects his daughter to observe the proprieties. The daughter of a sensible father is more than willing to meet these expectations. In the same way a sensible husband will expect his wife to see no more of the lover than "society" permits her to see of any man not related to her. No sensible American woman will jeopardize her good name under such circumstances. She will control her feelings until she has proved her new attraction and been duly released from the old. If a woman will not conduct herself in a self-respecting manner the sooner she leaves the better for the husband. As for herself, she will learn by experience—as Princess Louise did.

Love is the mightiest force in creation. It will not be gainsaid. But it can be controlled. To pen it up too completely brings explosion, devastation. To give it too free rein means madness with no less devastation. To *direct* it within reasonable limits is the only safe way.

It takes a cool head and steadfast heart to meet such emergencies as A.J.'s. And eye hath not seen nor ear heard the "Well done" and its attendant glory, which enters into the heart and character of the man who meets such condition and conquers—*himself*. Not once in a thousand lives has a man such opportunity to prove his godship and bless himself and the world.

Chapter IX: The Law of Individuality

All growth is by *learning*.

All learning comes by the gratification of desire. Truly, experience is not only the best teacher, but the *only* infallible one.

The gratification of desire, good or bad, leaves always one imperishable residue of wisdom. The rest of the experience goes with the chaff for burning.

Desire points invariably according to the individual's intelligence. In proportion as this is faulty his desires are "bad."

What *is* a bad desire, anyway? In the main "bad" desires are self-made or thoughtlessly accepted. Dancing is wicked to a Methodist and "good" to an Episcopalian.

But aside from these personal standpoints which are legion there is an immutable Law, to which intelligence is conforming all action and thought—the Law of Individuality—the Law recognized and expressed by Confucius and Jesus in negative and positive forms of the "golden rule"; "Do not unto others what ye would not they should do unto you."

Interference with the freedom of the individual is "bad"—that is, *it invariably brings pain* to the one who interferes, in thought or deed. Listen to this:

"You cannot know anything of the sources or causes of the crisis you are judging, for no one who knows will tell you, and you would not know if you were told. The depths of elemental immortality, of self-deceit and revenge, lie in our eagerness to judge one another, and to force one another under the yoke of our judgments. When there is the faith of the Son of man in the world, life will be left to make its own judgments. The only judgment we have a right to make upon one another is the free and truthful living of our own lives." George D. Herron.

This forcing of others, in mind or action, under the yoke of *our* judgment is the only possible way we can break a *real* Law. To be *ourselves* and to leave others free is to *"be good."* Dancing will come and go, and come again; so will fashions of all kinds; conventionalities and creeds; but this Law remains an eternal chalk line to be toed. And eternal torments await him who does not toe it.

Take the case of a man who desires to "run away" with another man's wife. The one immutable Law of Individuality says *no man owns a wife*. Instead of this being a problem with two men and one man's property as factors, it is a case of *three individuals* with god-given rights of individual choice. You have heard it said that *"where two are agreed* as touching anything it shall be done unto them." It takes two to make, or to keep made, a bargain. No matter what hallucinations in regard to ownership any man may labor under, *he does not* own a wife. He has no more "rights" over one woman than over another, or over another man, except as the *woman herself gives* him the right and *keeps on* giving it to him.

The Law of Individuality is absolute, and in due time husbands will know better than to imagine they own wives; wives will know better than to be owned; and the other man will not imagine he can gain great pleasure from "running away" with anything. Each will be free and leave the others so.

But "as a man thinketh in his heart so is he." Until a man *recognizes* the Law of Individuality his actions are governed by the Law he *does* recognize, and his desires act accordingly. When he desires to "run away" with anything his *conscience* tells him he is stealing. If desire is strong enough he steals a wife, and eventually suffers for it. For, though he may not have broken a real law, he *has* broken an imagined one and in his *own mind* he deserves punishment and in his own mind he gets it. "As a man thinketh so *is* he," and what he is *determines what he attracts.*

Never was a deeper, truer saying than Paul's *"Blessed is the man that doubteth not* in that thing which he alloweth." The man who *waits*, until he is *"fully persuaded* in his own mind" will be blessed in following desire, and he will grow in wisdom thereby.

The man who *thinks* his desire is "bad" and yet follows it, will grow in wisdom *by the scourging he gets*. He has transgressed *his conception* of the One Law and suffers in getting back to *at-one-ment*.

In either case he *grows in wisdom* and eventually he will desire only in accordance with the One Law of Individual Choice.

There is no question of "ought" about it. The individual is free to follow desire or to crucify it. And the fact is, *he follows desire when he crucifies it*. He *desires* to crucify desire, because he *is afraid* to gratify it.

The man who is not afraid follows desire and grows fast *in wisdom and in knowledge*. He may make mistakes and suffer all sorts of agonies as a result. But he learns from his misses as well as from his hits, and he progresses.

The man who is afraid to follow desire crucifies *his life* and stunts his growth.

It were better for the individual to follow his desire and afterward repent, than to crush his desires and repent for a lifetime under the false impression that the universe unjustly gives to another that which should have belonged to him.

There is just one kind of growth—*growth in wisdom*. We hear of children "who grow up in ignorance." We likewise hear that the earth is square and the moon a green cheese. Children can no more grow in ignorance than they can grow in a dark and air-tight case. *All* growth, mental, moral, spiritual or "physical," is by increase in in-telligence; i.e., by *recognition* of more truth. All things exist in a limitless sea of pure wisdom waiting, waiting *to be understood*. As fast as this universal wisdom is used it becomes *in-told—intelligence—* recognized wisdom. We *breathe in wisdom* and grow in intelligence. *All* growth, mineral, plant, animal, man or god, conscious or unconscious—*all* growth is by this process. It is *desire* that makes us breathe. Everything cries out for more,

more!—*it* cannot define always *what* it wants, but it *wants*, with insatiable craving. It is *more wisdom* the whole creation groaneth and travaileth to get. "Give me more understanding or I die!"—the visible eternally cries out to the Invisible. Desire is the ceaseless life-urge of all things, from amoeba to archangel. Desire is "Immanuer'—*God with us*—God *in* us to will and to do."

Chapter X: Harmony at Home

"I have recently married for the second time. My husband is a splendid man but his grown up children are not in harmony with me. Good people, but a different point of view. I make no pretensions to perfection, of course, but I do try to do the best lean."

This is the gist of several letters I have received from as many different women. I will answer them together.

When you enter a new home the matter of importance is *not* whether your new relatives harmonize with you, but whether *you* harmonize with *them*. It is for *you* to do *all* the adjusting.

This may seem hard, but it is not. It is an easier matter for one person to readjust her living than for a whole family to change. The family has not only its individual customs to hold each one, but its family customs as well; whilst you have left your family and have only your individual self to readjust. If you refuse to adjust yourself, for no matter what reason, you will act upon this family you have entered, as a red hot iron would act upon a pan of water—there'll be boil and bubble, toil and trouble and the family will fly to pieces. All because you came in with *positive* notions of your own which you insist upon enforcing.

But if you come into the family like a lump of sugar into a glass of water you will all, *in time* melt together and the whole family will be the sweeter and better for your coming. Whatever there is in you which is better and sweeter than their own ideas and customs will in time be *absorbed* by the family; for what is good is ever positive to the less good, and has a power of its own to convert; and every human soul, if left free, will eventually *choose* the good.

The only danger lies in your tilting your nose at *their* ways and ideas, and insisting upon your own. That rouses the sense of *individuality* in them and they then fight for *their* ways and ideas—then there's boil and bubble and sputter and flying apart.

Learn to vibrate *with* people where you can and keep still when you can't. *Look* for the little things you can enjoy together, and make light of the others. Recognize their *right* to differ from you, and *remember* that "*all* judgment is of God"—*their* judgment as well as *yours*.

All this differing of judgment among the people of earth is simply *God reasoning out things*. All the brains God has are your brains and mine. Just as in your brain you reason things for and against, wondering which is right and waiting for time and experience to decide; so God reasons one way through *your* brain and another and opposite way through *my* brain, and then rests and observes until the "logic of events" shall show *him*, and us, the point of real harmony. Just be still and *let* God think through your brain, and don't kick up a muss because he thinks out the other side of things through my brain, or your new relatives' brains.

Toleration is a great thing; but loving *willingness* to *let* God think out *all* sides of a question through all sorts of brains, is a glorious thing. Let's stand for our point of view when it is called for, but don't let's insist upon it. Let's remember always to use God's "still, small voice."

Do I need to tell you that what I have just said applies to you whether you have just married a second time or not? The whole world is our family, you know. Let's respect it and be kind to it, and *trust* it to recognize and appropriate our point of view just as far as is good for it. Let's be more interested in getting at the *other* points of view than insisting upon our own. That is the way we shall grow in wisdom and knowledge. And, too, that is the way we shall all get close enough together to really see the truth about things.

Chapter XI: A Mystery

"I desire to come face to face with the person or persons who are controlling and influencing my husband against his home and children and myself. He has been estranged from us all for several years, although sleeping under the same roof. Once I can find out the person or cause of his actions I can remove the effect, for I shall know just what to do. I want to solve the mystery."

The chances are you will never find that out, and if you did it would do you absolutely no good. Your husband is no dumb fool to be "influenced" this way or that by two women! He is a man with ideas of his own. If he was disappointed in you as wife, he has possibly turned to some other woman. If so the more you pry and suspect and hint around, the more positively he will turn away from you. If you "found out" and made things warm for him or another he would simply hate and despise you and be the harder set against you. This is the Law.

The thing for you to do is to recognize your husband's *right* to make and answer for his own mistakes. Then drop the whole thing from your mind and calculations.

Then treat your husband as you would any man who came to visit you. Make yourself as attractive and cultured and agreeable as possible, and look out for his comfort, but never get in his way nor question his doings. Stand square up on your own feet and be as fine a woman as you know how to be—as gracious a one. If he does love some other woman it may be but a temporary infatuation and if you are attractive and kind and sensible and independent enough he may return to his first love in his own good time.

If not, why, no matter. Just you get interested in life on your own account and let him do as he will. If he does care for another woman he deserves credit for not deserting you, as many a man would have done. Just respect and honor him for the good that is in him, instead of condemning him mentally because the good does not show just according to your ideas of how it should.

Love does not stay put, no matter how hard folks try to keep it put. All we can do is to be as lovable as possible and thus do our part to *attract* love.

It may be that you are simply a sentimental goose who imagines her husband is "influenced" away from her, because, forsooth, he does not pay her the attentions he used to.

I was once that kind of a goose myself, and it widened a breach that did not then exist except in my mind; widened it until at last it became a real breach—my husband went elsewhere for his companionship. I was too morbid and finicky and exacting for a healthy man.

Just as the husband of the woman in "Confessions of a Wife," in *Century* did. I read that serial each month and feel like shaking that little simpleton!—she is just the kind of a sentimental hair-splitting little idiot that I used to be! Instead of getting at her husband's point of view and enjoying *with* him, at least sometimes, she insists on acting the martyr because he will not dawdle around and gush at her feet.

Happiness and Marriage

Whatever is the cause of your trouble the only cure for it is Common-Sense. Live your own life, cheerily, happily, and enter into your husband's life so far as you can. Take all the good things that come your way and rejoice in them, but don't moon around and fuss because you can't have the sort of love-life described in some sentimental novel. Your business in life is to *love*, not to *be* loved. The latter is a secondary matter and the first is the thing that brings happiness to you. Go in to win now, and you can develop within yourself the full Life that you really desire. All you desire is yours and you will realize it in due time. But every moment you set your thought on straightening out Some Other body's life you are delaying your own realization and happiness.

Chapter XII: The Family Jar

"If a man and woman love each other and are every way suited to marry should they yield to the opposition of his grown daughter?" M.A.

This question in varying forms comes to me often. It always stirs within me something I used to call "righteous indignation." And incidentally it makes me smile. Translate the question into Plain English and anybody can answer it without hesitancy. Put it this way: When two Individuals know what they want and the whole world approves, should they go away back and sit down because a third Individual tries to interfere with their inherent right to the pursuit of happiness?

Of course *not*. A man or woman old enough to have a grown daughter is old enough to know whether he wants to marry again. Not even the most precocious daughter is a better judge than her father as to what is best for his own happiness.

Ah, there's the rub! It is not *his* happiness she is concerned about. It is her own. A new marriage would interfere with the daughter's plans. She would have to give the chief place to the new wife. She would have to give up a share of the prospective inheritance she has more or less consciously been counting upon. So she opposes her father's re-marrying.

But apparently not on these grounds—dear, no! Her father is "too old," or "too weakly," or the intended wife is "not nice." The daughter conjures up a dozen excuses, but never the *real* one; of which she is not fully conscious herself,—and *doesn't want to be*.

The parent's "duty" to children is great; far greater than the child's duty to parent; but parental self-sacrifice should certainly *not* be continued for life. A grown daughter is an Individual, who should stand on her own feet and make her own happiness *without* curtailing the happiness of parents.

Let her leave her father to a renewal of youth and happiness; or let her gracefully and kindly accept her rightful second place and use her loving energies in helping to make bright the home.

A sensible, well trained, loving daughter will do one of these two things.

A sensible, well trained, loving parent will consider his daughter's feelings and will do all he can to gain her *willingness* before he marries; but he will not make a lasting sacrifice of his own and the other woman's happiness simply to please a selfish girl.

If daughter and parent are not sensible, well trained and loving, it will be a case of frying pan or fire either way.

The recognition of individual rights to the pursuit of happiness according to individual desire, is the only basis of happiness in family relations.

The daughter who *helps* her father do as he desires will find *him* ready to help *her* do as *she* desires. And *vice versa*.

The daughter who "opposes" her father's marriage is quite apt to be the daughter who has *been opposed by her father*; he reaps as he has sown. Or else she is the daughter who has been brought up with the idea that parents are a mere convenience for her use.

The way out of the Family Jar is often labyrinthine; but the Loving Individual can always thread it.

Chapter XIII: The Truth about Divorce

In January *Psychic and Occult Views and Reviews* the editor, M.T.C. Wing, presents a view of "Wives and Work" which is anything but an *occult* view of the subject. He evidently still clings to the old notion that man was made for the family, and not the family for man. He inveighs against George D. Herron and Elbert Hubbard *et al* because they permitted themselves to be separated from their wives. Apparently he thinks the chief end of man is to tote some woman around on a chip, and the fact that in his callow youth man picked out (or was picked out by) the wrong woman, cuts no figure in the matter. Man must keep on toting her even if he has to give up his life work by which he has been enabled to supply the chip, not to mention the other things the woman demands.

All of which is the very superficial view of the world at large, and has no place among new thought, "occult" teachings. It is entirely too obvious—to the old-fashioned sentimentalist, who is blind to the real facts in cases of separation.

The sentimentalist gets just two views of the family, and draws his hasty conclusions therefrom. He sees first a happy family, a charming, clinging little simpleton of a wife, with half a dozen or so infants clinging to her skirts and bosom, and her round eyes lifted in adorable helplessness to the face of that great, strong lord and master, her husband. In his second view of the family he beholds this strong man turn his back upon this adoring family and walk deliberately forth to self-gratification, leaving them to perish from hunger and grief. Fired with these pretty and entirely fanciful pictures the superficial observer burns with indignation and calls down anathema upon the head of the deserter.

The fact is that *no* man ever deserts a family under such conditions. There is always a long period of disintegration before any family goes to pieces—a period of which *both* man and wife are well aware. When a separation comes it is *really* a relief to *both* parties. The only real pain in such cases comes from the spirit of *revenge*, or a desire on the part of one or the other to pose as injured innocence, that she or he may rake in the sympathy and fire the indignation of just such uninformed friends as M.T.C. Wing.

I have known a lot of people who separated—known them intimately and observed them well. In not one of these cases did the deserted party claim to *love* the deserter. In all there was a real *relief* when it was all over. In every case the one thing which had held them together so long was *fear of disgrace*. "Oh, *what* will people think of me?"—is the first cry of everybody— especially women. It was *that* which made the deserted one unhappy and resentful. It is that which makes many women pose as injured innocents and rate the deserter as a villain. And all the time *in secret* they are glad, *glad* that they are relieved of the burden of living with an uncongenial husband or wife.

Of course there are other reasons why women hate to be left by their husbands. One is that their support is apt to go with the deserter.

Public opinion keeps many a family in the same house years after it really *knows* it is separated widely as the poles.

The dread of having to take care of herself keeps many a woman hanging like grim death to a man she knows she does not love, and who despises her.

The fear of public opinion and the love, not of money, but of *ease*, holds together under one roof tens of thousands of families who have been *occultly* and really separated for years.

A man is held by the same sentimental notion that M.T.C. Wing has—that he must "protect" the woman. So he stays in hell to do it. He *has* to stay in hell *until she gets out*.

In almost every one of these separation cases it is the woman and *not* the man, who gives the signal. In George D. Herron's case the wife offered to take a certain sum of money and release him from supporting her. He met her conditions—and bore all the odium like a man. To her credit be it said she did not pose as an injured woman. I know nothing about Elbert Hubbard's case, but I venture to say that if he and his wife are separated that *she* was the one who did the leaving act.

We hear a lot about the "Biblical reason" for divorce; but I say unto you that infidelity is no reason at all for divorce. The one just cause for separation is *incompatibility of temper*.

A man is an Individual; a woman is another Individual; and neither can make himself or herself over to please the other.

When two people from lack of similar ideals and aims cannot *pull together* the quicker they pull apart the better it will be for them—and the children, too.

I know well a couple who lived together long enough to have grown children. For nearly a score of years they pulled like a pair of balky horses—what time they were not doing the monkey and parrot act. The husband stayed out nights and tippled. The wife sat at home and felt virtuous. Finally the woman worked up spunk enough to do what she had been dying to do for years. She packed up and left. Now she is happily married to a man she can pull *with*, And he is married to another woman who pulls with him. She has quit feeling virtuous and he has quit tippling. They are both prospering financially. The children have *two* pleasant homes, and more educational and other advantages than they ever dared hope for. Everyone of the family is *glad* of that separation.

The family is an institution of man's own making. It is a good and glorious thing so long as it serves to increase the happiness and health of its members. But whenever the family institution has to be maintained at the expense of the life, liberty or happiness of its members it is time to lay that particular institution on the shelf.

What God does not hold together by *love* let not man try to paste together by law.

One great cause of the increase of divorces is the financial emancipation of woman. Women can now get out and take care of themselves, where a few years ago they had to grin and bear it; or bear it without grinning.

If the new thought means anything, Brother Wing, it means that every individual man or woman, has the *right* to life, liberty and the pursuit of happiness wherever and with whom he chooses to seek it, so long as he or she does not attempt to abridge the same rights for others. It means that a woman is as much an Individual as a man, and must stand or fall, hold her husband or lose him, *on her own merits*. The new thought deals with Individuals regardless of sex.

Marriage is a partnership, subject in the eyes of Justice to the same rules which govern other partnerships. Let us be just to the deserter, be he man or woman, before we are sentimentally generous to the deserted.

And don't let us be *too* sure that we know all the facts in these separation cases. It is human nature to fix up outward appearances for the benefit of the passer-by.

Seek rather to *understand*. Condemn not.

Has any one told you it is lucky to be married?

I hasten to inform you it is just as lucky to be divorced, and I know it.

Chapter XIV: The Old, Old Story

This is the springtime, when fancy lightly turns to thoughts of love and everybody wants to go a-soul-mating. Consequently my mail is leavened with letters from those who are unhappily married but who are sure they have got their eye on the One who from the foundation of the ion was intended for them. They all want to leave the old mis-mate and go to the new found soul mate, and they all want my advice and encouragement—to do it! Some of these writers have already left their husbands (?) and want to know whether or not they should go back, or go on. To one such I wrote the following letter, which I publish in the hope that it will help others to find and follow *themselves*. Here is the letter:

One thing at a time! Get off with the old love before you go fretting about a new one! Don't you think you are a silly girl to ask *anybody's* advice as to whether or not you are to go back to your so-called husband? If *I* know what *you* ought to do I don't see what *you* are worth to yourself or the universe. The truth is that *you* are the only person in creation who can make that decision. If you don't yet *know* that you have a right to make your own life as you see fit; if you don't yet *know* whether or not you could go back to him; then *be still* until you *do* know.

You know things today that you did not know yesterday, and tomorrow you will know things you "can't decide about" today. So attend strictly to business and keep still, and stiller yet, until you know what is best to do.

Then *do* it.

So much for the old love. As to the new one, not even *you* can know for certain whether that other man would pan out the soul mate you now imagine him. But the Law of Love, or Attraction, will *prove* whether or not he is what you think. *Your Own* will come to you, and all creation can't hinder it If you keep that man was *not* what I longed for, a real comrade; sweet and cool, and free in your own mind, and make the best of *this* day as it comes along.

Ages ago I had a similar experience to yours. I found the only and original one intended for me. But I was tied to another man—*not* by a ceremony, for that ties nobody, but by my own conscience, which compelled me to "stand by" the man I thought "needed" me. So I stood, though I thought my heart was broken. In a few years I found that my soul mate was no mate at all!—I wouldn't have had him as a gracious gift! I felt like Ben Franklin who, as a barefooted boy, resolved that when he grew up and had pennies he would buy a stick of red striped peppermint candy; but when he grew up and had the pennies he didn't want the candy.

I have learned to smile at that experience as the bitterest and sweetest of my past life, and the source of volumes of wisdom. The *Law of Attraction* knew and the Law kept him from me. I afterward found the real comrade, and *more* than the joy I thought I had forever missed!

"We are pretty silly children, dearie, without the child's best quality, *trust*."

Just you *let go* of everything and everybody and apply yourself to doing *this* hour, with *love*, what your *hands* find to do; and trust the Law to bring you in due time *all* the good things you ever desired.

Accept what comes as *from* the Law; meet it kindly and do your best.

The time came when I left my husband and secured a divorce. This may be your time to leave, or it may not. But *no* one can know but yourself, and you will know as soon as you really *want* to know what is *right*, and get quiet enough to find the decision *about which you have no doubt.* "*Blessed* is he that *doubteth* not in that thing which he alloweth." "He that doubteth is *damned already*." When you are *sure*, then go ahead; and the whole universe, seen and unseen, will work together for you and with you.

What is it that ties you to one man and not to another? Not the words of a priest or a justice of the peace. It is *your thought* about the matter, and *his* thought about the matter, which ties you. You may not have thought you were tied until the preacher told you; but not his words but *your acceptance* does the real tying.

If you are ever freed from a husband you must *think* yourself free—just as you must think yourself free from any other bondage. I thought myself free several years before I applied for a legal separation; so that when I did apply it was to me merely a technicality.

Divorce or no divorce you are *tied* to a man until you think yourself untied.

Be still and find your mental freedom. Then you will know what to do.

A year after I wrote the above letter to a young woman who wanted to leave her husband and go to her "soul mate," I received from her another letter in which she thanked me from her heart for my letter, which, she said, had saved her from a terrible mistake. She had let time try the new love; who was found sadly wanting. More than that she had come to love and respect her husband as never before. Many others, both men and women, have written me to the same effect.

Can you learn from the experiences of others—learn *caution* at least? I hope so. Be *sure* you are right before you resort to separation.

In the meantime make it the aspiration and business of your life to know *that* all *things are* now *working for good to you and your mate, and all you hold in common.*

Keep sweet, dearie, and *let* them work—at least until you know exactly *what* to do, and *how* to do it; and can feel *sure* in your heart of hearts that, *whatever the consequences,* you will never regret your action.

www.ingramcontent.com/pod-product-compliance
Lightning Source LLC
Chambersburg PA
CBHW021916160426
42813CB00096B/132